JETS AND BOMBERS ACTION

by M.L. Williams

**All photos by
United States Air Force**

Published by Willowisp Press, Inc.
401 East Wilson Bridge Road, Worthington, Ohio 43085

Copyright © 1990 by Willowisp Press, Inc.

All rights reserved. No portion of this book may be reproduced, stored in a retrieval system, or transmitted, in any form or by any means, electronic, mechanical, photocopying, recording, or otherwise without prior written permission from the publisher.

Printed in the United States of America

10 9 8 7 6 5 4 3 2 1

ISBN 0-87406-471-6

CONTENTS

The F-16 Is Always Ready to Fight! 4
The F-5 Is a True Freedom Fighter 6
The Thunderbirds Show Their True Colors 8
The F-16 Out-Maneuvers Its Competition 10
The Navy's Blue Angel 12
Supersonic Speed—The B-1B Bomber Has It! ... 14
The B-52 Can Really Travel 16
The B-1B—Aerodynamics in Action 18
The FB-111 Bomber—It Can Float 20
The F-14 Tomcat Can Land on a Ship! 22
World Speed Record Holder—
   The SR-71 Blackbird 24
Spy Planes Know It All—
   The RF-4C Phantom II 26
The F-15 Eagle—It Performs 28
The RC-135 Can Handle
   Top-Secret Missions! 30
Glossary 32

The F-16 Is Always Ready to Fight!

This awesome F-16 Fighting Falcon can reach 1,600 mph (Mach 2) at 40,000 feet. The F-16's bubble canopy cockpit allows the pilot to look ahead and up without anything in his line of vision. Not many F-16 pilots get caught off guard by the enemy during air combat.

The F-16 is a favorite in the USAF because it can make really sharp turns at great speeds. It can out-maneuver just about any other fighter around!

The F-5 Is a True Freedom Fighter

The F-5 Freedom Fighter is a supersonic fighter! It can reach speeds of up to 925 mph. This plane can take off from a normal airport runway or off of an aircraft carrier.

The F-5's missiles are carried on the jet's wing tips and cannons are carried in the nose of the Freedom Fighter. This plane can handle enemy combat with no problem!

The Thunderbirds Show Their True Colors

Check out the U.S. Air Force Air Demonstration Squadron, the Thunderbirds. The Thunderbirds use red, white, and blue F-16 Fighting Falcons as their official aircraft. This incredible group of jets performs about 85 shows every year. During their half-hour performance, the Thunderbirds perform 36 unbelievable maneuvers. It's a thrill to watch the squadron of F-16s in action!

The F-16 Out-Maneuvers Its Competition

These three F-16 Fighting Falcons fly in formation as they perform a training mission. This fighter aircraft's excellent handling and speed are part of the reason that the F-16 has the best safety record of any single-engine fighter in USAF history.

The Fighting Falcon has nine stations for carrying weapons. The fighter can be ready for combat in the air when it is outfitted with air-to-air missiles. It can also be used to attack enemy targets on the ground when it carries air-to-surface missiles.

The Navy's Blue Angel

The F/A-18 Hornet is both a fighter and a bomber. It can reach speeds of up to 1,350 mph (Mach 1.7) and can accelerate vertically straight up in the air! The Hornet in this photo is getting ready to launch off of a CVN-69 aircraft carrier. The Hornet can take off from ground bases, too.

The F/A-18 is one of the U.S. Navy's newest jets. It's the official aircraft of the Navy's flight-demonstration team, the Blue Angels. Like the F-16 Fighting Falcon, the Hornet has great maneuverability so it can perform fantastic stunts for the Blue Angels!

Supersonic Speed—
The B-1B Bomber Has It!

This soldier is reporting to the radar tower that his B-1B bomber is prepared for a quick takeoff! The B-1B carries out strategic air missions. B-1Bs attack with bombs behind enemy lines and target things like military bases, factories, and ports. These attacks are

supposed to hurt the opponent's ability to fight.
  On July 4, 1987, a B-1B set international speed and distance-with-payload records. The payload is the total weight of the crew, fuel, weapons, and supplies that an aircraft can carry.

The B-52 Can Really Travel

The B-52 Stratofortress is a long-range bomber. The first B-52 was built in 1954, and the bomber is still in use today. It can carry up to 20 missiles, and it supports other aircraft on strategic bombing missions.

This bomber can reach speeds of up to 650 mph! The B-52 has eight engines. It can travel for more than 7,500 miles without refueling. Since the Stratofortress can fly for such long distances, the plane usually only stops when the crew needs a rest. The crew is made up of six—the pilot and co-pilot, two navigators, an electronics warfare officer, and a gunner.

The B-1B—
Aerodynamics in Action

Before a plane takes off, it must have a thorough flight check to be sure that it does not have any mechanical problems. These men are up early to prepare the B-1B for a practice run.

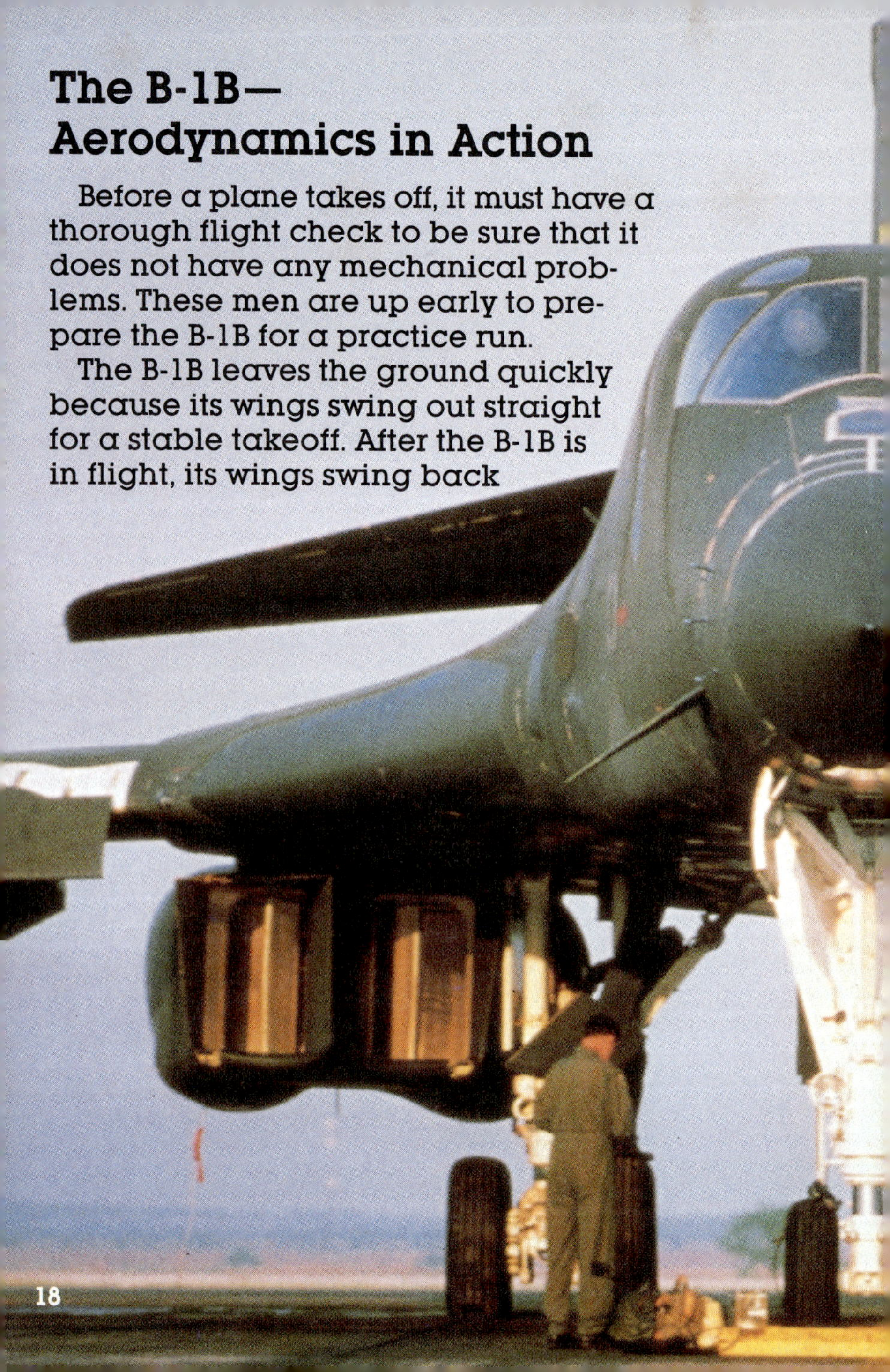

The B-1B leaves the ground quickly because its wings swing out straight for a stable takeoff. After the B-1B is in flight, its wings swing back

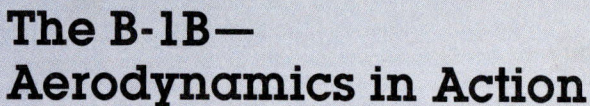

so that the bomber is more aerodynamic. The top speed of this strategic bomber is 1,100 mph (Mach 1.5), and its normal cruising speed is 530 mph.

The B-1B can fly at high speeds at low altitudes in order to bomb enemy targets. Check out the B-1B's four powerful engines in this photo.

The FB-111 Bomber—
It Can Float

The FB-111 is a medium-range bomber. This bomber can fly twice the speed of sound at altitudes from 35,000 to 60,000 feet!

The FB-111 has a crew of two—the aircraft commander and the navigator. If the crew must eject during an emergency, the bomber has a special explosive cutting cord that separates the cockpit module from the rest of the plane. After the cord is cut, the module heads toward earth by parachute. There are airbags attached that help to cushion the fall, and the unit floats if it lands in water. After landing, the module serves as a shelter for the crew until help arrives.

The F-14 Tomcat Can Land on a Ship!

The F-14 Tomcat is a huge twin-engine fighter. It operates off of a U.S. Navy aircraft carrier. The F-14 is designed to attack air targets that threaten its home ship and other ships that may be traveling with it. The Tomcat must land on its aircraft carrier's steel deck at a high speed. To land, the pilot must head for four steel cables that are stretched across the flight deck. These cables catch the plane as it heads in for a landing, and the fighter quickly comes to a screeching halt!

World Speed Record Holder— The SR-71 Blackbird

The SR-71 Blackbird has broken many world speed records. This awesome spy plane can reach speeds of more than 2,000 mph (Mach 3) or 3,100 feet per second! The SR-71 is powered by two jumbo turbojet engines, and it is very hard to catch if chased by enemy planes.

The SR-71's special camera can take a picture that covers 125 miles in one shot. Its cameras are so well focused that the pictures it takes can show a person's face from 10 miles away! The Blackbird takes pictures of things like enemy ships, military exercises, and aircraft for U.S. intelligence agencies.

Spy Planes Know It All— The RF-4C Phantom II

The RF-4C Phantom II is an unarmed spy plane, officially known as a reconnaissance aircraft. The RF-4C carries high-tech, electronic radar sensing devices and cameras to detect and photograph enemy military movements and bases. It is able to carry out its spy missions during daylight and at night. The RF-4C performs well in any type of weather.

The RF-4C has two crew members—one sits behind the other. The pilot sits in the front seat and the radar systems officer sits in the back. The RF-4C flies at speeds of up to 1,600 mph (Mach 2). Its high speed is this plane's only defense against enemy aircraft.

The F-15 Eagle—It Performs

The F-15 Eagle is a powerful force in the USAF! The Eagle is a tactical fighter. Its main purpose is to fight air-to-air combat. It can outperform and outfight just about any enemy aircraft in the world—at any time of day or night and in any weather. The Eagle can reach speeds of more than 2,000 mph (Mach 2.5).

The Eagle has a crew of only one pilot. The fighter's awesome electronic radar system gives the pilot the ability to track other aircraft that are up to 100 miles away.

The RC-135 Can Handle Top-Secret Missions!

The RC-135 Reconnaissance Aircraft is a finely tuned reconnaissance, or spy, plane. The plane does not carry any weapons. Instead, it carries lots of special computers, radar devices, and cameras. This equipment can supply the USAF and the U.S. Department of Defense with pictures and information about foreign military bases.

GLOSSARY

Bomber. A bomber's job is to drop missiles or bombs onto enemy targets.

Fighter. A fighter does one or more of these things: fights in air-to-air combat, drops bombs or missiles onto ground targets, or defends against bomber attacks.

Mach. Mach numbers are used to describe the speed of planes that fly near the speed of sound. Mach 1 (740 mph) is the speed of sound and Mach 2 (1,480 mph) is twice the speed of sound. The speed of sound changes at different altitudes with the air's humidity and density.

Payload. The payload is the total weight of the crew, fuel, weapons, and supplies that an aircraft can carry.

Reconnaissance Aircraft. A reconnaissance, or spy, plane flies over enemy territory. It carries special computers and cameras to supply the military with information about enemy bases and troop and ship movements.

Subsonic. Subsonic is a term used to describe flight speed that is slower than the speed of sound.

Supersonic. Supersonic is a term used to describe flight speed that is faster than the speed of sound.